Dear Cheryl,
Great meetin'
all the bes[t]
future endeav[ors]
very be[st]
Nancy W.

TOLERANCE
101

Practical Solutions for
Interfaith Problems

Foundation for Religious Freedom
1680 N. Vine St., Suite 415
Los Angeles. CA 90028

Phone: 800-556-3055 or 323-468-0567
Website: www.forf.org

The Foundation is a 501(c)(3) tax-exempt, non-profit corporation.

The printing and distribution of this booklet by the Foundation is funded through donations.

All donations are tax deductible.

Discounts for purchase of bulk copies are available.

We hope this booklet is useful in promoting tolerance and mutal respect.

We would very much appreciate your feedback if you find it helpful.

By Nancy O'Meara and Stan Koehler

Nancy O'Meara volunteered on a national interfaith hotline for over two years, personally answering more than 5,000 calls and helping people resolve situations involving deep belief differences.

Stan Koehler teaches conflict resolution at Columbia, University and also volunteers in a New York prison program helping inmates restore their self-dignity to enable them to start life anew after making their amends to society.

Publisher's Cataloging-in-Publication
(Provided by Quality Books, Inc.)

Nancy O'Meara & Stan Koehler
Tolerance 101 : practical solutions for interfaith
    problems. -- 1st ed.
        p. cm.
        ISBN: 1-928575-04-8

        zxxx1. Religious tolerance. 2. Freedom of
religion. 3. Religious--Relations. 4. Cults.
5. Toleration.   I. Foundation for Religious
Freedom.

BL640.T65 2000   291.1772
                                    QBI00-375

INTRODUCTION

We don't know if it happened on the 500th or 5000th call. But somewhere amongst the thousands of phone inquiries to the Foundation for Religious Freedom's Hotline it became obvious that a common sense handbook is needed on how to handle "cult" situations.

The Foundation is a tax exempt, non-profit organization dedicated to bringing reason, truth, and understanding to an often explosive subject: the involvement of oneself, a friend or loved one in a group that some might call a "cult."

We don't criticize or endorse any one religion. We have people from many diverse faiths on our board and acting as professional referrals. **Our service is free.** We promote honesty, dialogue and mutual respect. We are passionate about the First Amendment and the power of communication to sort out religious differences, keep families together and relationships intact.

You may have heard a shocking story about a group your family member has joined. Keep in mind, newspapers and tabloid television news give the world sensationalism. The public is subjected to the shocking, the bizarre. What isn't made clear is that the lurid tales, though sometimes true, are in fact, rare. It is not often realized that a skewed picture is being shown or that some of these incidents are the acts of individuals and have nothing to do with any group.

It is like covering the subject of Motorcycle Racing but only showing pictures of crashes. Yes, smash-ups do occur in the motorcycle world, but that's not the whole story.

Our hotline **(1-800-556-3055)** rings daily with calls from people worried about the fate of a friend or loved one in a group they've never heard of or about which they have only negative information.

This handbook covers the common-sense advice we give those callers. We have included many real-life stories from our files to illustrate that families and individuals DO overcome serious religious differences and to show how innovative people can be in accomplishing such.

One of our key tenets is that people should find out for themselves and make up their own minds. This handbook is full of ideas on how to do so.

We hope you find it both practical and thought-provoking.

The Foundation for Religious Freedom contacts of experts and help groups is constantly growing. Please write, use our website, call or e-mail us if we can be of assistance.

Very best,

Board of Directors
Foundation for Religious Freedom
www.forf.org
1-800-556-3055

CONTENTS

SECTION ONE
WHAT TO DO WHEN SOMEONE YOU LOVE
JOINS A GROUP YOU THINK YOU HATE

SECTION TWO
WHAT NOT TO DO

SECTION THREE
SPECIAL CATEGORIES

APPENDICES

What to do

when someone you love joins a group you think you hate

CALM DOWN

STAY IN COMMUNICATION

GET MORE INFORMATION

OH NO! WHAT HAS HE DONE? WHAT DID I DO? WHY

DID THIS HAPPEN? OH NO! WHAT HAS SHE DONE?

WHAT DID I DO? WHY DID THIS HAPPEN? OH NO!

WHAT HAS HE DONE? WHAT DID I DO? WHY DID

THIS HAPPEN? OH NO! WHAT HAS SHE DONE? WH

DID I DO? WHY DID THIS HAPPEN? OH NO! WHAT HA

HE DONE? WHAT DID I DO? WHY DID THIS HAPPEN?

CALM DOWN
(breathe)

Sit down.
Take a deep breath.
Think it through.

Do not panic.
Don't over-react.

Overreacting to
a person's life
choice is certainly
a fast way to
alienate them.

The smart thing to do as a first step is take a deep breath and calm down.

You don't know the whole story yet.

Calming down does not mean doing nothing. It means getting your thoughts together and acting rationally.

Calm down means just that. **Calm down.**

After you have taken a few deep breaths and given yourself time to think about it, you can contact the person you are concerned about and talk to them intelligently.

Then go forward from there — getting more information, making sound decisions and taking sane actions.

This is not overly simplistic. It is sensible.

How many situations have you seen mishandled because of an undue emotional reaction based on incomplete or sensational information?

9

example #1

A Midwest couple never thought it would happen to them. They had raised their daughter to be sensible. The young woman graduated from business school in Florida.

Then came the news.

At age 23 she joined a youth-oriented Christian church that has had more than its share of negative publicity.

The parents feared for her well-being. They imagined all manner of things happening to her. They reacted with a plan. They would swoop down to Florida, "snatch" their daughter from the group and haul her back home. It seemed the right thing (the necessary thing) to do.

But was this really a sensible response to the first time their 23-year-old daughter made a life choice they did not agree with?

Amidst the height of their turmoil, the parents called our hotline. They were helped to realize the "snatch" plan might possibly teach their daughter a wrong lesson about thinking for oneself and freedom of belief.

Instead they took the trip to Florida, visited the church their daughter had joined, talked over their concerns and found out for themselves what the group was all about.

The result? The daughter moved back to the Midwest with her parents where she has much better job opportunities and now attends the local branch of her chosen church.

example #2

A woman in New Jersey became frantic after repeated phone calls to her brother-in-law in Los Angeles produced no response.

She knew he was a vegetarian but had recently discovered he was also a Hindu and planning a trip to dark, dangerous India where who knows what might befall him. Maybe he had already been kidnapped.

She was counseled to calm down. She was informed that they do have running water and electricity in India and persuaded to leave a caring but concerned message on her brother-in-law's answering machine. Finally, she was advised not to offer him hamburger.

Did her worst fears materialize? Not quite. It turned out the man, who worked as an animator, was 100% safe and sound, but was literally sleeping at the office to meet a production schedule.

IT'S SO NICE TO HEAR FROM YOU! I'D LOVE TO

KNOW MORE ABOUT THE THINGS YOU'VE BEEN

DOING. DO YOU THINK WE CAN TAKE SOME TIME TO

TALK THIS WEEK? IT'S SO NICE TO HEAR FROM YOU! I'D

LOVE TO KNOW MORE ABOUT THE THINGS YOU'VE

BEEN DOING. DO YOU THINK WE CAN TAKE SOME TIME

TO TALK THIS WEEK? IT'S SO NICE TO HEAR FROM YOU!

STAY
IN COMMUNICATION

The importance of communication cannot be over-stressed in a situation with deep belief differences.

Re-establishing communication after it has been severed can be a monumental if not sometimes impossible task. It is much wiser to keep a connection no matter how extreme the upset might be at first.

It is vital for communication as a concept to be understood. The word derives from the Latin, **"communicatus"** - from **"communicare"** (to impart, share, literally — to make common). Thus it can mean a sharing of beliefs to gain understanding.

Communication does not mean a one-way flow of ideas from you to the other person in which you tell him all that is wrong with what he believes; how he has disappointed you; how he has made the wrong choices or how much more correct your own beliefs are.

Communication is not a confrontational diatribe, not a denigration of the beliefs of another. One of the definitions of communication is synonymous with "dialogue." Dialogue includes the flow of ideas back and forth between people, really listening to the other person and trying to assume the other's position and understand his viewpoint.

The challenge is respecting the other person's right to a point of view diametrically opposed to one's own and really hearing what he has to say. This includes not mentally negating what another says before he even says it. It also means not planning your rejoinders to each of the other person's points and then spouting them in an unstoppable judgmental stream.

If a person you know, respect and care about has done something that does not make sense to you, it is highly likely that you are missing information. The way to get that information is through communication.

Maybe the information will not be something you want to hear, maybe you will find it theologically abhorrent. If you are a religious person, you may fear for the person's soul or spiritual fate. These can be matters of considerable anguish.

Nonetheless, gone are the days when blasphemers and non-believers could be locked away or stoned. We live in an age when all adults have inalienable rights to life, liberty and the pursuit of happiness, no matter how new and different those pursuits might be. This of course does not include illegal pursuits.

It is up to you, not the other person, to initiate and follow through on dialogue. Let's say your sister has found something she is happy with. If you do not understand it, then it is you who needs to ask questions and get your concerns addressed. Be non-judgmental but honest about your worries. Set aside a specific time to ask these questions (not accosting her at a sibling's birthday party or Mom and Dad's wedding anniversary).

If you foresee a possible volcanic eruption, invite someone else along who is good with a fire extinguisher.

Throughout your conversations and exchanges, make sure you are not part of the problem or making it worse by your approach. Straightforward questions with no pre-conceived expectation of the answers will go a lot farther than slanted barbs that imply you've already made up your mind before you've even heard the replies.

The person may say things that sound strange to you at first. Be patient until you fully understand. Remember, people who believe quite differently from each other can still see truth, hope and a chance for a better world through practicing the beliefs which they embrace. The great cultures of Egypt, China, Peru,

Greece and others presented a vast spectrum of religious concepts yet each enriched humanity.

What's the point of coming across negatively? A rejecting message from you about another's beliefs can be very alienating. Say some-one tells you how fantastic classical music is, how it lifts him to a higher appreciation for life. You respond by saying it's rubbish and that most serious music composers died broke or of venereal disease. Would it then be a surprise if he should want your influence out of his life.

No matter how different someone else's beliefs are from yours, all their likable qualities (sense of humor, appreciation of books or movies, the way they can make strangers feel at ease) are still there. The person who loses is you, if you force them to stop communicating with you because you are so right and they are so wrong.

Take care in being too critical. Great religions of today started out tiny and often reviled. The size and current popularity or impact of the person's group is no measure of its ultimate future on the world's stage. Mormonism, Islam, Christianity and Buddhism were all originally "cults" to those who could not look through the telescope of history to see whether these belief systems would blossom or fade.

By all means, express your views. Certainly, express your concerns. But in doing so, try to avoid being so fixed in your ideas or so prejudging that you are unable to communicate fairly and sensibly.

In family situations where you are twice the age of the other, you might find it hard to respect his right to believe as he wishes. After all, you have lived so much more of life. You have seen much more. You have had experiences the younger person can learn from by listening to you. However obvious that may be to you, it just might not be the way the other person looks at it.

In fact, he might think you have accepted information without questioning it. He might think your values and belief system are the cause for all that is wrong with the world — rather than the cure.

This can be disturbing. We often assume that all of our kind and kin will think and believe as we do or meekly revise their incorrect views when we point out to them the errors in their thought processes. The history of the human race tells us otherwise, however.

So you must communi-cate. **Honestly.**

If you want to under-stand why the person has become involved in such a group, then say so. Say "I do not understand how you became involved in Spiritual Light. Can we have dinner this week and talk about it?"

On the other hand, if you had heard about the group and wondered if it might be of interest to you, then be honest about that, too, and tell him you are interested for yourself. With sincere communication you may be surprised to learn something about the one for whom you care so much that you never knew before. It is not unusual to be very close to someone without ever deeply discussing the spiritual side or questions of faith.

The point is to be compassionately, not cruelly, honest. Tell the person what you have heard that worries you. Allow him to respond. You may be surprised at how much sense his answers make.

Communicating and staying in touch might be difficult if one person is hundreds or even thousands of miles away. In that case, phone calls, letters and e-mail are, of course, immediate remedies. Best is arranging a personal meeting even if it might be some time up the road. With real communication you will be able to understand why the other person made his choice. It doesn't mean you will agree with that choice. If you don't, use it as a character-building experience (understanding someone while completely disagreeing with him). The person who can do so is a rare diamond amongst the myriad gems of humanity.

Do not sever the communication. **Keep it alive.**

examples #3-4

One mother was worried that her daughter, who had moved in with a small elitist community, would not be able to talk as freely as she had previously.

The situation was handled simply by providing a cell phone which the daughter keeps with her twenty-four hours a day.

Mom may not like her daughter's religious choice, but she stays in touch and knows her daughter is OK.

An elderly woman in Southern California was trying to trace down her middle-aged son who was living with a remote communal group in Alaska. The group is very rustic with no phones or electricity.

Through a number of phone calls to the closest small town, a communication line was established with a pastor who arranged to visit the man and relay the message of concern from Mom.

The return message explained that her son was safe, was sorry for not staying in touch and was doing well living the life he feels is best for him. The pastor has continued to act as the relay point so both people's wishes are respected.

examples #5-6

A Catholic parent was concerned with the fact that his son had fallen in love with a Mormon woman. He wanted to know what he should do.

Since both the son and fiancé were in their early twenties, the advice given to Dad was "Invite her over for dinner."

Dad got the point — lessening by one the many challenges the young interfaith couple will face in creating a successful marriage.

A woman in northern California had a pagan son who had met and become engaged to a Wiccan (a "good witch") via the Internet, moving to rural New York to marry his fiancé without ever having met her face to face. Mom was not financially able to pick up and fly east, and despite many phone conversations, really wanted someone to go meet the fiancé for her.

After a number of phone calls a local Catholic priest was found who was willing to act on the mother's behalf.

He made a friendly visit, met and had dinner with the young couple. He was happy to tell mom that her new daughter-in-law was part of a peaceful religion, relieving her fears.

IF THE COMMUNICATION HAS BROKEN DOWN — FIND A WAY TO FIX IT

It might be extremely difficult to reestablish the connection if it has already been severed in a now regretted overreaction to the situation. There are many, many ways to reestablish communication. Easiest is probably a heartfelt apology, honestly admitting you were wrong to prejudge.

If a direct approach is not possible, then there is always the option of using another family member to act as a via. You can also use a mutual friend, a pastor, rabbi, a teacher whose class you both attended, anyone who you both know who would be willing to help. There are also professional facilitators you can hire to contact the other person and negotiate for you.

If the situation is across a long distance, local groups can be contacted — interfaith groups, local police, local ministers, local mediators — that can help re-establish communication.

Few people feel good about not talking to their own family. In by far the majority of cases you will be able to persuade them, somehow, to stay in touch and respect your right to think and believe differently than they do as long as you do the same in return.

Be persistent and creative and you will find a way.

examples #7-8

Despite arguments and pleas, one young woman could not get her mother to see that her religious choice was a permanent change, that she was never going to become the "rich lawyer's wife" Mom had dreamed of.

She finally wrote a note to Mom in which she apologized for any hard feelings she had created, then explained how much she loved her parents and was proud of the way they had raised her to think for herself, trust her own choices and be true to her own spirit.

They built on that apology, and today have a loving relationship, despite a very wide doctrinal chasm.

One woman's adult son became involved in a fundamentalist group, which "officially" had an open door policy that was in actuality played down to the point of the group becoming exclusionary in practice.

Mom took the open door policy seriously and went to see her son at the group's international teaching center, taking both him and an instructor to dinner. She didn't stop there, but ensured she was given a tour of the facility, during which she asked intelligent questions and saw that she got to know people in the group personally.

She has kept in close touch with her son and become a regular visitor, making it clear through her actions that while she understands others might think she was of the devil, she didn't believe so, and has as much a right to her beliefs as they do to theirs.

example #9

Two middle-aged sisters living in Texas had ended all contact over a disagreement in Catholic theology and were refusing to allow their children (cousins) to see one another. The parents of the sisters were divided on the issue as well, not knowing who to side with.

The older sister was adamant that a resolution was needed, if only for the sake of the children. She was provided help by a Buddhist (and professional mediator) who volunteered to work with her to resolve the situation.

Many long phone calls were invested into sorting things out until the true cause — a third person who was covertly saying bad things about each sister to the other — was spotted.

The result? They made an agreement they could all live with, and the whole clan — including parents, sisters, nephews and nieces — had their first family Thanksgiving dinner together for years.

EXTREME

CASES

IF YOU CANNOT LOCATE A FAMILY MEMBER —
HIRE A LICENSED INVESTIGATOR

If the family member has a social security number, has been in contact with any of his friends, has established a way to receive mail or phone calls, has set up an e-mail address, has opened a bank account, has gotten a job, or many other things, a professional can locate them and assure you of his or her safety. Possibly that professional can open communication to see if the family member wants to be in touch with you. If the person does not want to communicate with you, at least you will know he or she is safe.

examples #10-11

Several years ago an East Coast couple had an adult daughter who not only disappeared physically, but got word to the parents that she never wanted them to find or contact her.

Needless to say, the parents became extremely anxious. They paid a private investigator to locate her.

He found the woman had moved west and become a member of a motorcycle group. It was what she wanted out of life but felt her parents would never understand her decision. The private investigator convinced her to let him tell the parents she was safe.

To this day he is their go-between for information, keeping the parents informed that she is well and passing on their messages.

After an Arizona man's wife disappeared with their four-year-old son, he discovered her diary. It expressed very unique religious convictions, including something he interpreted as possibly suicidal.

He immediately obtained competent professional investigatory help, while sending copies of the diary to several religious experts who advised him that her thoughts did not seem life-threatening. His wife and son were found in California alive and well.

Though the marriage wasn't saved, through the legal means of the court system, Dad now has full visitation and an excellent relationship with his son.

WHAT IF YOU ACTUALLY FEAR FOR A LOVED ONE'S LIFE?

What if all attempts to establish communication have been unsuccessful and you have reason to fear for another's life?

You must call the proper authorities. Call the local police or the sheriff's department.

A policeman showing up at the door of some out-of-the-way place, politely inquiring about the whereabouts of a person who was last known to be at that location and asking to please see the person to ensure their health, is a way to ensure the safety of the person.

Use only legal means.

Recognize that an adult does have the right to live a life totally different than the one you expected them to. But you can ensure that they are living such a life safely and of their own choice without violating any laws or their civil rights in any way.

YOU MAY THINK YOU KNOW ABOUT A GROUP

because you have heard or read about it in the media or because an ex-member wrote a book about it, or you met someone in the group years ago.

Would you consider that someone could understand your religion after one conversation with an ex-member? Have you ever seen a newspaper article that really delved into the theology of a religion?

The group and its theology probably contain a lot more than you can learn from such cursory contact.

Go after the information with an open mind. Don't assume you already know all about it and then just look for information which confirms what you already "know." What could be more boring?

GET MORE
INFORMATION

Treat it instead with a spirit of learning. Something new to understand. Do people really believe that way? Someone I know is
involved with this — what do they see in it? Approach it that way
and you'll find it fascinating.

DIG A

LITTLE DEEPER.

GET A BETTER

UNDERSTANDING.

IT WILL BE

WORTH IT.

GET CURRENT INFORMATION

Religious groups are not static. Their membership changes. Their interaction with the rest of society changes. Sometimes even their theology changes. Find out what they really believe and practice today. There are many, many ways to do this. The following are some ideas that have been tried and worked.

A. CALL THE GROUP DIRECTLY

It is amazing how many people who have questions do not call groups directly. The repeated refrain is "the group will only say good things about themselves." Well, that may be true, but if someone said bad things about you, wouldn't you want them to ask you if they were valid? At least give the organization itself a chance to state its case. Getting information directly from the group does not preclude you from obtaining information from other sources.

Who tells the world the virtues of corn flakes? Who provides the information about how important milk or eggs are in one's daily diet? *Those who sell them, of course.* Yet after reading all the nutritional notes on your box of cornflakes and seeing the milk mustaches on the most beautiful and best, one can still pick up health-food store literature covering the similarities between cardboard and corn flakes, the dangers of cholesterol, lactose, too much animal protein and why being a vegetarian is the best dietary choice of all.

Call the group yourself and ask for their information packet — they should be more than happy to send out free information in the mail which can be read at one's leisure. If the group is not willing to do so, that could be an indicator which should raise a little mental red flag. (It could also mean they are not financially sophisticated enough to have information packets.)

example #12

A man living in infamous Waco, Texas, "...where we know about cults," had gotten word of a group operating south of him — Angel Lightning and his boys.

The man was on his way to abduct one of the "boys" out of Angel's group, positive that Angel was holding them against their will.

After some firm persuasion the man heeded the apparently novel idea that he should go meet Angel and his followers before passing judgment.

Imagine his surprise when he discovered that Angel and his gang of grown-up men (all in their thirties) were actually former criminals who did voluntary carpentry work to help needy families.

Call our hotline
(1-800-556-3055)

B. IF THEY ARE DISTANT —
CALL THE GROUP'S 800 NUMBER

Many groups have 800 numbers. Call them. Explain that you are concerned and why. Ask them questions. If it is a small group, then they might know right away that you must be the relative of their newest convert. Be prepared for that and be up front.

If you are not satisfied with the way the person on the 800 line is responding to your questions, say so, and ask if you can talk to a supervisor or person who has had more experience. Whatever failing you are finding in the person's answers, tell the supervisor and get a response. Be persistent and get your questions answered. If they have an 800 number you can bet that it is supposed to be there so people can get their questions answered. Get them to do so.

At the same time, be polite.

The person at the other end is answering questions from a person she has never met and about whom she knows nothing. Good manners from you will certainly elicit a more complete response than a threatening or superior attitude.

Finally, don't assume one individual is completely representative of the organization or its policies. Talk to someone else or several people. Surprisingly, sometimes the people on the phones are inexperienced or very recent members. Talk to a higher-up or someone who has been involved for years before making a judgment.

C. GO VISIT THE GROUP

Almost all spiritual groups encourage more membership. Most have some type of public information events — lectures, open houses, Sunday services, potluck suppers, etc. Going to such an event and actually meeting members of the group is a great way to form an opinion based on firsthand information.

D. ARRANGE A SPECIFIC MEETING

Call up the local branch/chapter/church and tell them you know someone who has become involved with their organization and you want a meeting. Meet with them yourself, ask your questions, get a tour of the facility, check it out.

E. MEET GROUP MEMBERS SOCIALLY

Make it a point to meet members of the organization in a setting which is outside the religious context. One very influential religious freedom advocate used this as his way of personally finding out about new religious groups. He would find out which local store was owned by someone in a certain new religion, which office manager was a member of a new religion, etc. and "happen" to meet them. He got to know them as people — an activity to be emulated.

F. IF IT IS ON A COLLEGE CAMPUS, CALL AROUND, YOU CAN GET UP-TO-DATE INFORMATION

Universities often have ombudsmen, or student affairs departments or even religious affairs offices. Make some calls to the university and you should be able to locate someone knowledgeable and helpful. They will be able to answer your questions about how the group operates on campus, should you be worried, and if so, why? They should also be able to give you the name and number of the local representative of the group on the campus so you can talk to them directly.

G. TALK TO A MINISTER OF FAITH YOU KNOW

Talk to a minister you respect about your concerns. If it is a local group, a local minister almost certainly will have heard of it, maybe even met some of the people at community events. See what he knows, what he has heard about them, what does he think your concerns, if any, should be.

If it is a group in a distant location, you can call directory information for that town and ask for the number of a local church which is a denomination you are familiar with. Talk to that pastor. Find out what he's heard and what he knows.

H. TALK TO A PROFESSOR

Religion professors all over the country have done studies, read or written papers, etc. and are knowledgeable about a wide array of groups. Often sociology professors or history professors are as well. Call your closest institution of higher education and get the name of such a person. Leave a message on his or her voice mail, saying when you can be reached. You can count on a fascinating conversation with someone who often has a real insight.

I. VISIT THE GROUP'S INTERNET WEBSITE

Most groups have their own web site where you can read up on what they have to say about themselves, at whatever time of day or night is convenient.

J. VISIT AN INDEPENDENT WEBSITE

There are many excellent web sites which give objective, factual information about diverse groups. They include controversies but at the same time give both sides of the story. Sites which are connected to universities, sponsored by interfaith organizations and ones which clearly state the authors of the information (such as a religious studies scholar) are worth your time to read.

K. WHAT ABOUT NEGATIVE WEBSITES?

Negative sites are out there about everything from Hindus to Jews, Buddhists, Pagans, Catholics, Scientologists, Fundamental Christian groups, ad infinitum. The common denominator of most of the sites is that they are created by ex-members. This information is dicey at best. One has to consider motives. It is similar to asking a divorced person about his or her ex. You may get the truth, you may not. There's a good likelihood you will get a lot of drama about how "no good" he or she was.

Most ex-members depart their groups under neutral circumstances. But a few leave with vengeance on their minds and can be quite driven about it. The simple fact that these websites are pronouncedly negative, even alarming, should alert one that he is not getting a full story that presents the pros and cons. But sorting the fact from the fiction can be difficult.

If a site comes across as if the former member were a "victim," that should sound an alarm. Some people do not seem to see themselves as victims of their own choices in life, but victims of someone else. Rather than taking an experience and using it to grow and learn, some become embittered and blaming. When you come across a website by such a person, make sure you take it for what it is worth.

L. WHAT ABOUT ANTI-CULT WEBSITES?

There are also sites that list hundreds of "destructive" groups, or only negative things about totally diverse spiritual/self betterment/religious groups. Check out who is writing the stuff, who is funding it and what their agenda is. If it is a former deprogrammer who has now become an "exit counselor" recognize he is a person who was paid for violating basic human rights of freedom of conscience. If that's your kind of guy, you are reading the wrong handbook.

The Oxford Dictionary defines cult as "a particular form or system of religious belief." If the site defines "cult" as a group which controls the member's lives and dictates their actions then you are getting more propaganda than truth. That is the psycho-babble definition of religion. It stirs up fear in people. It also violates common sense. Which religion does not teach a moral code — thus dictating to some degree what the members do or do not do? What religion doesn't demand certain times of the week for devotion, prayer, or re-dedication of one's spirituality — thus controlling the member's time to some degree?

Religions and betterment groups which are actually trying to make the world a better place generally do expect certain moral standards in life and relationships. They have done so for thousands of years. Find out who is writing or sponsoring any "cult or anti-cult listing" website — it should either be right there on the site or quickly available by e-mail. Evaluate the contents of such accordingly.

M. USE YOUR LIBRARY

Books or publications are available about many groups. Take the time to pick some up and read them yourself. The best will have actual interviews or speeches or writings of the founder, spiritual leader, originator, guru or teacher. Scholars who really study the theology, organization, history and many other facets of religious groups have written very objective books and papers. They have real jobs and often their research is funded by a university. They will include the controversies, but at the same time be balanced.

Students of religions around the world would agree that much has been done in the name of almost all religions that would never have been sanctioned by the founder of the religion. So criticizing isolated aspects of the organization rather than the actual aims and goals of the founder or original leader is a lazy way to evaluate a religious organization. What dreams did the founder envision for the group? This will tell you about the group's intent.

N. WHAT ABOUT NEGATIVE BOOKS?

If you *do* read negative books, check
out the author's agenda. You may
have to read between the lines.

*Former member kicked out
20 years ago after failing
to live up to the moral
standards of the
group?* Does the
book include the
court documents
detailing how much
he asked the group
to pay him for not
publishing his book?

*Person who joined the group "undercover" and was never honest
with the group about his intentions or why he was there?* Now
writing about the group's duplicity?

Ex-daughter-in-law of a "charlatan" posing as a religious leader?
Does the introduction to the book include how much money she
accepted from the subject of her disillusionment as a cash
settlement or how many thousands she is accepting from him
every month in child support?

*Arm-chair critic with no better answers of his own, trying to make
a name for himself by interviewing only people with negative opinions
and calling that research?*

**Be more discriminating than to buy books like these and give
such people royalty payments.**

O. TALK TO THE LOCAL POLICE

Groups spring up all over America for weeks, months or even years and are then never heard of again. These range from small branches of national groups to people who channel the Virgin Mary and start their own  following. If there is anything illegal going on, the local police will be the first to know. If there are any questions about what is really happening, a neighbor has likely called in to complain, even if only because too many cars were parked in the street. The police have probably checked it out. If the group you are worried about is in a far city, you can still get the name and number of the local police there and get in touch with them. Local police are the ones who would also be the first to know if anything truly dangerous (such as illegal drug use) is going on and would be the ones to ensure such a possibility is correctly dealt with.

P. FIND OUT IF THEY ARE FOR PROFIT, NONPROFIT OR TAX-EXEMPT

A for-profit organization is just that — it is involved in making a profit for its owners or share holders. Some self-improvement seminar organizations out there are profit-making companies — overtly so. That is relevant information.

Then there are nonprofit groups. Anyone can start an organization as a nonprofit group.

This means simply that it is not incorporated for the purpose of making anyone rich, but for some other reason. Nonprofit is not the same as tax-exempt. Tax-exempt means the group has shown evidence to the Internal Revenue Service which satisfies legal requirements that it is operating in a way that benefits others so that people who donate funds to the organization can take tax deductions for their donations.

Q. GET COPIES OF THEIR INCORPORATION AND TAX RETURN DOCUMENTS

Legitimate groups have no problem sending out a copy of their Articles of Incorporation which will include the stated purpose of the organiza-tion and signatures of their Board of Directors. If the Chairman of the Board is a preacher, and the rest of the Board consists of his wife, his daughter and son-in-law, that may be legal. But even better would be a Board consisting of the preacher, a local bank manager, and local high school principal. Whatever the case, it is information that can be used in determining the quality of checks and balances within the corporate structure.

Churches are not required to file tax returns with the IRS and few do so.

Similarly, religious organizations (worshipping congregations, associations of such congregations, "intergral auxiliaries") are tax exempt, per se, and are not required to apply to the IRS for recognition of that status. However, most such groups do so primarily because it makes their life easier with a variety of other transactions, including state and local exemptions, charitable groups, etc. When the IRS grants such groups their exemption from tax, the IRS informs the group whether an annual tax return is required.

So you can ask the group if they file IRS Form 990 (the number of the annual tax return for a non-profit organization). If they do, the documents are a public record, so they should have no problem providing a copy of the most recent, or even earlier years.

If they have not filed a 990 it is no reflection on their legitimacy as a religion or religious association.

R. LOCAL INTERFAITH ORGANIZATIONS

Contact a local interfaith group which will very likely have someone who has met with the group and knows about it firsthand. Talk to such a person directly. Find out what his own belief system or value system is so that you can include that information in your assessment of what he tells you about the group you are inquiring about.

examples #13-14

A woman from Canada, deeply alarmed at her 30-year-old daughter's decision to join a "new age" community in the US, was convinced to make a long trip and visit the group herself. Much to her surprise, the group is a peaceful, ecologically-oriented communal organization including many professional people.

After learning the facts, the woman fully supported her daughter's involvement.

And her daughter has now been happily living there for over two years.

A man in his late twenties planned to move into a very strict communal group in the Midwest. Mom was more than a little worried.

Convinced to go visit the group, she found out she really liked the people there and that her son could not have chosen a better environment. He was in a supportive situation where he would be able to spend the maximum of time on the work he loved (making stained glass windows by hand), while others did the baking, cleaning and mending that he hated.

As she said, "He's chosen a simpler life. He's not going to be watching a lot of television and he's never going to have to worry about the chlorine level of his swimming pool."

examples #15-16

A Lutheran woman could not believe her niece was giving up a college scholarship to travel in Russia. She was adamant that the niece be stopped from such a foolish course and had stirred up Mom and Dad against the young woman's decision.

After many phone calls finding out exactly who the group was that the niece had become involved with, the family decided that attending a non-denominational Christian missionary school, and then traveling to Russia to witness and work could in fact be an incredibly spiritually enriching experience for the young woman.

A woman from rural upstate New York described a group who had purchased a property near her farm. They wore turbans, long white robes and many did not speak English. She had concerns of possible violence from such a group, even though her portrait sounded like a group which is adamantly anti-violence.

The handling? Following some simple advice, the woman baked a pie, drove to the neighbors, told them, "Hi, I'm your neighbor. How about some coffee?" and got to know them.

Call our hotline (1-800-556-3055)

examples #17-18

A woman in southern California was concerned about a church moving into her neighborhood. It had an ethnic make up different than her own congregation and already had a large following in a nearby town.

Actually going to the services of the church, speaking to the people attending, meeting the pastor and finding out about that Church's programs was a brand new concept to her. But she liked it and applied it and found out she even liked them — despite their "incorrect" theology.

A woman from northern California felt desperate to extract her son from a church group which had possibly abducted him. She was especially stressed because she knew her son had a serious drug abuse problem.

Further investigation quickly ascertained that her concerns were based on false information. In reality the group was a Baptist-funded drug-free rehabilitation ranch where the clients are also taught life-skills.

The son could not have been in better hands and Mom sure had a change of heart about "cults."

THE MEDIA: CONTROVERSY VS. HATE SPEECH

The seemingly easiest way to get more information about a religious group would be through mainstream media. In actual fact, it's probably the worst.

Why is mainstream media so unreliable about religious or spiritual issues? The media's job is controversy and sensationalism — opposing views, blood, sex, big names, big money — that is their stock in trade. Proof of this is the hundreds and hundreds of religious groups that start up, operate for years, and then disappear never to have been heard of in the media. Small churches all over the country are headed by local ministers who have their own congregations, work hard at their job, serve their community, raise a family, minister to the elderly, comfort grieving relatives, perform christenings and generally help people live worthwhile lives. You won't hear about them in the papers, except for a small mention in the local daily when the pastor dies.

When was the last time you saw the headline: "Religious Group Does Good Works"?

Many members of the media will readily admit that they have no religious beliefs of their own or have not practiced any religion for many years. Trashing people's religious views is not too difficult if you have little empathy for the spiritually-minded. Unfortunately, religious news stories don't include any disclaimer or footnote such as, "I really don't have any spiritual grounding and was only assigned this story because there were no good rapes or murders that day." If such disclaimers were noted, we may discover the journalist, upon finding no controversy to report, dug around and found that one member of this group had worked for a famous movie star and was convicted of stealing money from that star, who later died a gruesome bloody death. The reporter then found a way to weave all that irrelevant information into a story about an eastern mediation group's program for helping foster children. Voila, we have a headline.

Reporters, radio producers or TV producers can be quite cynical. Many do not believe that anyone is well-intentioned or wants to help others. You can test this for yourself. Call a newspaper and talk directly to a reporter who has done a negative piece about a religion or self-improvement group. Ask the reporter what his religion is. He does not have to answer you but will probably not hesitate to tell you "none" — and does not even see the incongruity — he's just a reporter. Then ask him if he is involved with anything that is trying to make things better: Big Brothers, Scouts, mentoring? Ask him what contribution he does to his community for a purely altruistic reason. Get an answer. Then you'll have a better understanding of this fellow. You'll see how he can irresponsibly quote the "critics" of betterment groups who themselves have rarely done anything helpful to others with their own lives but have no trouble getting their names in the media as critics.

example #19

The media latched onto a **satire** some years ago about the "TNEVNOC" cult, written by two famous sociologists (Anson Shupe and David Bromley).

The sociologists explained how the Tnevnocs pry young female virgins away from their families, cut their hair, change their names, enforce a cannibalistic ritual of drinking the blood and eating the flesh of their dead leader. They even perform a wedding ceremony to him, placing a gold wedding band on their third left-hand finger, and force the young women to lie prostrate, humbling themselves to his will.

Tnevnoc is "convent" spelled backwards.

Call our hotline
(1-800-556-3055)

What NOT to do

consider this rule carved in stone

Don't ever pay someone to talk anybody out of anything. No matter how worried you are about them, no matter how wrong you think their choice is, no matter how dangerous you think the group is,

Don't pay someone to talk them out of it.

Why?

The practical reason is because hundreds (if not thousands) of qualified professional people all over the country will help in such a situation for **absolutely no charge.**

- There are ministers who will talk to loved ones, who will share their faith and the reasons they hold that faith, rather than negate the value of other beliefs.

- There are hundreds of religious studies professors in universities who are willing to speak to the family member.

- Dozens and dozens of interfaith organizations have knowledgeable people who will be more than happy to help.

- Attorney firms have expert mediators who will do mediation work for free.

- People who make their living as facilitators in dialogue will sometimes help for free in an emergency.

This is one area of life where there is an abundance of qualified people who will go out of their way to help for no charge.

The higher moral reason to etch that rule in marble is called **the Golden Rule.**

Would you want someone else to hire a professional hate speaker to rail against you for several hours due to your "wrong" faith choice?

The deeper human-rights reason is because **the people who will do this kind of thing for money to their fellow man** — *harangue, harass, invalidate, evaluate, demean, belittle and criticize beliefs* — **are people who took a very wrong turn in their life path some time ago.**

They are not intent on helping, or they would become
mediators or facilitators.
They have no better ideas
of their own, or they would be
writing books about such.
They are not highly successful, or they would be too busy
with productive living to be
involved in something so
debase. They are not the
kind of people you would
want leading your child's
scout troop or playing in your
bowling league. **Don't hire
them. Don't use them.**

**Find someone you know and
trust who will honestly help
for no monetary return.** If you don't know such a person, get
someone you trust to help you find such a person.

One scary reason is because in the past the people who have done
such things were factually criminals (with police records) and
performed illegal abductions, often with horrific results. Adult
family members who were illegally kidnapped commonly refused to
communicate with the family for years and even after reestablishing
communication never felt the same about their parents or fully
trusted them again.

OK, HERE'S THE FIRST PAYMENT. IT'S ALL I HAVE RIGHT NOW BUT I KNOW I CAN BORROW SOME FROM MY (FATHER, BOSS, WHATEVER) AND GET YOU THE REST IN A WEEK. AND YOU PROMISE ME YOU'LL MAKE SURE

THAT HE WILL BE GLAD TO BE BACK HOME WITH US WHERE HE BELONGS! OH WHAT A RELIEF! I DON'T HAVE TO DO ANYTHING BUT WAIT FOR YOU TO DO IT! THIS IS WONDERFUL. IT'S WORTH EVERY PENNY!

THREE

SPECIFIC DON'Ts

DON'T PAY FOR A DEPROGRAMMING

Deprogramming is virtually unheard of in America today. *Thank goodness.* Most people find it hard to believe it was ever practiced in the past few decades. In its heyday, deprogrammers described their service in numerous ways to make it sound like something other than it really was: **a brutal, dehumanizing violation of basic human rights.**

The victim was held against his will, commonly after being abducted. Then he or she was emotionally and spiritually assaulted in an attempt to cause him to recant his beliefs. Sometimes the person was physically assaulted — *handcuffed, tied down, beaten, raped and denied food, sleep and water.*

After several high profile deprogrammers were jailed or fined millions of dollars in damages, this practice was discontinued in the United States. The most infamous US case was a criminal deprogrammer from Arizona who was fined $2,500,000 in 1995 for "acting in a way that is so outrageous in character and so extreme in degree as to go beyond all possible bounds of decency and to be regarded as atrocious and utterly intolerable in a civilized community." Reports of such brutalities continue to surface in other places around the world. A desperate person taking desperate measures that he knows are wrong is not going to achieve a right result. You won't find anyone who is not a criminal who will *do* a deprogramming today. **Kidnapping is a felony.**

example #20

I n the late 1980s, during the height of deprogramming mania, with reportedly hundreds of criminal abductions happening a year, a dismayed Jewish couple, convinced of the "evil" of their daughter's religious choice, paid for the deprogramming of the daughter and her husband. The 24-hour abduction included being driven to a remote cabin by a lake with no way back except via the 4-wheel drive driven by the abductors.

The incident had only one long-lasting result: complete alienation of the adult daughter from her parents for many years.

Despite the parents recanting their actions and making it right with God via atonement, it was only after several years, and the birth of a grandchild, that a loving relationship was restored. This is typical of "deprogramming" attempts.

Call our hotline (1-800-556-3055)

DON'T PAY FOR AN EXIT COUNSELING OR INTERVENTION

Exit counseling seems to have sprung up after the court system caught onto the barbarisms of deprogramming. Exit counseling apparently has no rape or physical violence connected to it. It simply involves hours of belittling and picking apart the beliefs of another human being.

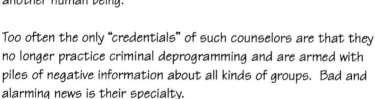

Too often the only "credentials" of such counselors are that they no longer practice criminal deprogramming and are armed with piles of negative information about all kinds of groups. Bad and alarming news is their specialty.

Today's exit counselors will demand that a family member be present at all times during the browbeating. (Having a family member present seems to prevent physical violence.)

Exit counselors will not warn those thinking of hiring them that exit counseling has a very low success rate. They will not present any kind of legal contract guaranteeing a result or return of funds for failure to achieve such. Nor will they disclose that exit counseling often makes the situation worse than ever — the adult raised on the principals of freedom of conscience finding it almost impossible to forgive his own family for being so vicious.

One's own minister, a school counselor, a mutually respected friend who will sit with you and your loved one together, helping your concerns be communicated rationally, and ensuring that the responses to your worries are also listened to — this is a much more successful way to sort out situations.

example #21

As recently as 1997 one mercenary haranguer (exit counselor) agreed to talk to a woman whose father was absolutely adamant she leave a fundamentalist Christian group. Before beginning the confrontation an agreement was made of just how long the de-conversion would last.

With no result at the end of the agreed upon time, the father tried to convince the exit counselor to continue.

He refused to do so — but didn't return one penny of his fee despite only making the situation worse.

Call our hotline
(1-800-556-3055)

WHAT ABOUT A "VOLUNTARY" INTERVENTION?

The difference between voluntary and involuntary intervention seems to be the finest of lines.

Theoretically, a voluntary intervention involves an adult agreeing to allow a stranger to badger him for hours about his religious choice.

Voluntary interventions seem to occur after considerable pressure is brought to bear by the parents, compelling their offspring to agree to listen to a critical diatribe for an exactly stated period of time.

Normally the stranger has never had a meaningful conversation with the "intervenee." Nor does he have any concept of how the person came to his choices. He doesn't ask if the person he is speaking to has found the organization beneficial or if he has warm friends in the group. The paid verbal abuser commonly has no spiritual path himself. What seems to matter is that he knows all the negative stories about the organization he is criticizing.

It is an unlikely way to build family relationships: hiring someone no one in the family knows to spend hours pounding his own interpretation of truth into someone who doesn't want to hear a word of it.

You do not have the option of doing anything illegal, even if you are convinced that the adult you care about is on a wrong-headed freeway ride to unhappiness.

That is because you live in America. In order for you to exercise the freedoms that you have you must allow others to practice those same freedoms.

You factually cannot legally physically stop an adult from making an unwise job choice, making a bad investment that you are sure is a scam, running around with people you totally dislike, marrying the "wrong" person or choosing a religion you completely disagree with.

If you could, then anyone could also stop you from your choices. It's not just a slippery slope, it's an ice-coated sheer plummet.

So what you do is communicate. You care. You continue to be a friend and family member.

You write. You send letters, packages. You send photos.

You let the person know you love them, even if you disagree with some of their choices. One day they may change their mind and need your help. One day you might change your mind and realize that it might not be the life for you but they are happy.

Most of all, you grow. It is about life in a pluralistic society. You grow because you find out that the deep aspects of the person you love are still there no matter what their belief choices. Their zest for life. Their sense of humor. You both still have similar situations to face in life as spouses, as parents, as voting members of a republic.

Maybe because of the person's religious choices there will be behavior changes that you don't like. You have a right to communicate about such while respecting their privilege to make those choices. Common sense advises, of course, that you not communicate about such in a way that is demeaning or ridiculing. Although questioning someone's religious notions is fair play, tact and manners are usually needed to lubricate the uneasiness of such inquiries.

You may be quite firm in your own beliefs after considerable pondering. Perhaps your certainty is based on logic. Perhaps faith is the foundation. Whatever the basis for belief, the area of religious faith is much more nebulous than, for example, the laws of science. Disproving another's views can be as difficult as proving one's own.

Be intelligent. Be responsible. The religious freedom practiced today is unparalleled. You must practice it yourself if you want others to practice it with respect to your own beliefs. The richness of diversity is a wealth we all share.

example #22

ver twenty years ago, a young woman made a choice to join a controversial and zealous religious community. She married within her chosen faith, a family oriented religion. Her mother cut all communication to the daughter and enforced all other family members do the same.

The young woman is not so young now and has four children of her own. Her mother recently wanted to know what her daughter's religion was "up to," as the estranged daughter had tried to contact Mom.

Mom rebuffed the attempted reconciliation, as "my daughter made her choice."

Of course, grandma has that right. She also has other grand-children.

The children of the ostracized daughter have no other maternal grandmother or access to aunts, uncles and cousins on Mom's side. All that potential love has been taken out of those lives because of grandma's disapproval of mom's religious choice.

DON'T LISTEN TO
ANTI-RELIGIONIST HATE SPEAK

"Mankind is composed of two sorts of men," wrote Cuban author and patriot José Martí a century ago, *"those who love and create and those who hate and destroy."*

We have all felt vengeful at one time or another after an unhappy experience. Children are particularly prone to this. But one of the signs of maturity is learning to examine bad experiences and see where we are responsible or what went wrong. We then proceed to learn from such and see what can be done constructively to improve.

Successful marriages grow through spouses who learn from their spats and try to responsibly better their own behavior as well as their partner's. Those who choose the opposite path — complaining, blame and revenge — usually end in divorce.

In all aspects of life, we find those who solve problems with a positive attitude and those who attack their troubles destructively.

Religion is no different. People sometimes have negative experiences with churches or decide they dislike them or find their practices or beliefs peculiar. Most folks take this in stride. But a tiny handful do not. These small numbers engage in hate campaigns with no constructive purpose (other than the obliteration of the group or groups they rant about).

Consider a simple analogy:

*A man suffers very painful food poisoning after eating bad chili.
He is irate.*

- He contacts a lawyer and files a negligence lawsuit on the restaurant.
- He checks out chili further. He discovers that chili actually has had other reported cases of food poisoning — especially if the red beans are not cooked for the right length of time at the right temperature.
- He creates a chili victims group called "RBCGY — Red Beans Can Get You."
- He puts up a Website, does radio talk shows, does television, writes an alarming book containing statistics that absolutely prove the dangers of chili.
- He goes on the lecture circuit as a victim who survived and lived to tell about it.
- He becomes famous. He makes lots of money.
- He is awarded the first annual "Chunky Soup Humanitarian Award".
- Chili cook-offs are banned.
- Chili consumption plummets.

Another man is painfully food-poisoned after eating chili. But he takes a different approach. Instead of automatically blaming others, he finds out what happened.

- He gathers facts, learning the beans weren't cooked long enough or at a high enough temperature.
- He informs the manager of the restaurant what happened and makes sure needed changes are immediately made so no one else will get chili poisoning at that restaurant.
- He checks out chili further. He discovers that the importance of cooking red beans at the right temperature and right length of time is known but has been completely left out of the local restaurant inspection regulations.
- He contacts the correct restaurant regulating authorities, takes the right steps and ensures that the regulations are changed as needed.
- He puts up a fact-filled Website, does radio shows, gets other groups to support his activities so that a similar clause is included in city restaurant inspection regulations far and wide.
- He watches in satisfaction as the reported number of food poisoning cases from chili drop dramatically.
- Chili consumption soars.

Which man would you like as your neighbor, friend or co-worker?

While it is true that a few isolated instances of real danger have occurred in minority religions, actual harmful practices are quite rare.

Those who specialize in panic and danger warnings about any non-mainstream group need to be looked at hard and long.

One has to ask: What exactly is the danger they are warning of? Are they concerned that other thought might be introduced into our society?

Are they proposing that the ideas of the past and present must never be challenged? Are they pounding a message of hate and intolerance for new ideas? Do they fear you will stop thinking for yourself — or how they have decided you should think?

Two thousand years ago would they have been the ones railing against the message of Jesus to love thy fellow man?

A few hundred years ago would they have been the ones preaching against the value of people with different skin pigmentation or with a different slant to the eyes?

In more recent years would they have been the voices spouting platitudes about the weaker sex, while insisting ladies be kept from the voting booth, executive board rooms and institutions of higher learning?

Real hate mongers usually aim at emotionally charged issues to stir up animosity. They may make claims that a group "brainwashes," takes money, breaks up families, enforces sexual rituals — all manner of ideas that will strike a nerve. They will even pass these on to the media.

But on inspection the statements often turn out to be half-truths or twisted truths, if not altogether false. (These falsehoods can sometimes be cleverly convincing if you don't bother to investigate them.)

A comedy television show once featured a grieving mother who wanted her adult son deprogrammed because he was in a "cult" where he was "not allowed to marry, forced to wear black and to live on a diet of crackers and wine." The punch line: *the son came on stage and was a Catholic priest.*

If you do come across alarming news about a group, make an effort to delve further. Ideally, go to the group and observe firsthand what they do and believe.

The man who yells fire because he sees smoke and feels the heat is not the same as the man who yells fire because he suspects all strangers are arsonists.

Know the difference and make your decisions accordingly.

WHAT ABOUT EX-MEMBERS?

Most of us are ex-members of some
religious group or groups. We did our
stint and went onto other things. We
may think about the experience
now and then with good, bad,
or indifferent feelings. We
may or may not still have
friends from those times.
That is the vast majority of us.
This is, by far, the lot of most
ex-members.

Then there are those who are quite bitter about their experiences.
Who knows why? If they are responsible for their bad times, we will
probably never know because they will almost certainly feel and say
that others are to blame. The vocal critics of new religious groups
are frequently sour former members.

Some have had a bad experience with one organization and have
turned it into a generalized hysteria about all religious groups.

Modern communication technology has made it easier for such birds
of a feather to find each other and flock together. A few displeased
former members of religious groups have banded together to form
their own support groups. While this may briefly help a few who want
to blow some steam, the downside is that such gatherings tend to
do little that is constructive.

They also perpetuate downtrodden attitudes in the members.

There is a better way.

66

If an ex-member has had a bad experience, our time-tested advice is:

A) Make an effort to do something effective to change whatever was wrong (writing letters to the management of the group, demanding a meeting with such to get your issues fully resolved, actually getting it sorted out for good), and

B) Get on with life. Life is too short (or depending on your religious views, this life is too short) to spend giving in to feelings of hatred. Such things fill one's days with darkness. Get on with life.

WHAT ABOUT THOSE WHO PREACH ABOUT THE FALSE THEOLOGY OF OTHER RELIGIONS?

Religious groups vary tremendously in their tolerance of other ideas.

Some encourage members to study other doctrines freely, seeing this as an expansion of the individual's understanding of others and the world.

At the other end of the spectrum, some groups shut the door on any beliefs but their own. They may forbid members to read books or enter churches of other faiths, or they may routinely speak disparagingly of other beliefs. They may preach against "false religions."

Such, of course, falls within the rights of all religions. They protect or warn their members as they see fit. It is also, of course, natural for religious people to see their views as "the one true religion."

Through upbringing or study or both, most conclude they are right and others are wrong.

However, it is one thing to reject another man's faith — to honestly point out its flaws and failings by one's own standards. Reject it if you must. Call it a "false theology" if that is how you see it. But how far can we sensibly take this? Do we now reject the person, too? Do we advocate hatred of his group? Do we condemn all association with him?

The claim of "false religion," while understandable, has a tendency to lead us across the threshold of intolerance. It is probably more human nature than religious doctrine to belittle those different from us.

Unfortunately, this can take us into deliberate slander or spreading of falsehoods about other faiths to make them look bad in contrast to "the one true religion."

It is not our place or desire in this book to undermine those faiths who preach against "false theologies" or "false religions." Rather, on this subject we appeal to all to keep in mind what may be the most universal religious doctrine of all: **"Try to treat others as you would have them treat you."**

Even if others disagreed with you, you would likely want them to treat you civilly. You probably would not want them to spread lies about you or your religion. You would no doubt want them to make an effort to judge you and your beliefs on facts, not rumor or twisted reports. Nor would you want to be deprived of rights because of what you believe. Even if others saw your theology as strange, you would still want them to remember that you are also human and feel the same pain as they would if they were ridiculed or ostracized.

A more constructive use of one's religious message might be to attack the real enemies of religion everywhere, such as:

Despair.

Hopelessness.

"Experts" who say that man cannot change.

Educational establishments that nullify ethics or morals.

Teachings that chemicals alone can heal troubled spirits, hearts and souls.

A man with a calling can use his voice, his pulpit, his standing to lift people to a better, more responsible life. *Such men of faith and goodwill are simply too few and too valuable to have them not work together.*

Setting the example starts in one's own back yard. If we want others to respect our views, common sense would indicate we need to show the same courtesy.

example #23

 Lutheran pastor married a woman whose father is an active Mason.

The minister had heard Masons had evil beginnings and made it his personal mission to discover and expose their dark underbelly.

Twenty years and hundreds of hours of research later, he published an anti-Mason book. No great revelations about illegal activities or lives shattered or homes wrecked. Little about the charitable works or positive aspects of the Masons. Just a lot of bad news. He got even more in the bargain.

The pastor has alienated himself from his father-in-law. His son has lost a grandfather. A grandfather whose "sin" was to belong to a group who thought differently than the pastor.

example #24

O ne Southern California Christian minister has "investi-gated" and written a book about four other faiths and their "false" theologies. He details what is wrong with these other faiths. He lectures about this. He prides himself on this knowledge.

But is he really treating others the way he wants to be treated?

Not really. He is a Baptist. One of the most disturbing facts of life for him should be that his faith is viewed as a destructive cult in Belgium and France.

Special Categories

TEENS, CULTS & ILLITERACY

BRAINWASHING & MIND CONTROL
— THE HOAX

DIFFERENT IS NOT DANGEROUS

WHO WINS WHEN RELIGION
LOSES

IT'S OK TO JUDGE —
USE THE RIGHT CRITERIA

DO SOMETHING ABOUT IT —
EXPAND YOUR HORIZONS

I KNOW YOU'll FIT RIGHT IN WITH THIS GROUP.

I THINK YOU HAVE A LOT IN COMMON WITH THEM

AND IT WILL BE SO NICE TO SHARE IT WITH YOU .

I KNOW YOU'LL FIT RIGHT IN WITH THIS GROUP.

I THINK YOU HAVE A LOT IN COMMON WITH THEM

AND IT WILL BE SO NICE TO SHARE IT WITH YOU.

I KNOW YOU'LL FIT RIGHT IN WITH THIS GROUP.

TEENS

CULTS & ILLITERACY

Today's multi-cultural society makes it easier than ever for young adults to encounter widely diverse theological teachings.

Teenagers have a natural curiosity. They are approaching adulthood. They have an urge to test the waters of independent thinking. This can be a source of great concern for parents. It's a troubled world out there. Exposing our kids to it can feel like letting puppies loose on a busy street. At first we leash them, of course. But in the end they are not puppies. They are, and let's not forget it, young men and women. Just as we all once were.

So what do you do when they want to know about the Hari Krishnas they saw on the boulevard? Maybe you panic. Maybe you foresee losing your child to tambourines, shaved heads, and orange robes. Should you tell your teen vague, bad things about this group to scare them off? Should you tell them what rumors you heard about the Krishnas that make them look bad?

You may have plans for your teen's life. Dreams of them entering missionary work or of a life following the beliefs they were raised with. So when you find them reading a book on Buddhism or scanning the Internet for information on witchcraft, what **DO YOU DO?!?**

It can be a nervous moment. And for teens it can sometimes be a decisive moment. **Think before you act.** When you were young, was there a time when you questioned the faith you were raised with?

Were you curious about what other people believed? Did you ever have a desire to find "the real truth" about God, the after-life or man's soul?

How did you feel when you were allowed to think for yourself and come to your own conclusions? And how did you feel when someone insisted you "stop that nonsense" of questioning such things?

Parenting is an awesome responsibility. Your belief may be — as it is with many mothers and fathers — that you have an obligation to insist your teen go to your church and study the teachings of your religion. And the thought of your son or daughter rejecting your faith could be heartbreaking.

On the other hand, you may feel it is your job to see that your teenager, on the brink of adulthood, is allowed to make up their own mind.

Regardless of your views, it is important you be honest with your teen. If you tell them biased or vicious things about other beliefs, they may find out differently. Then who is the bad guy, you or the Hindu guru you vilified — who, it turns out, encourages truth-telling?

Be honest.
Be sensible.

Tell them your misgivings if you have any. By all means, tell them your own way of judging right from wrong and your own spiritual grounding. But use common sense. **Pushed too hard, teens often do the opposite of what we want.**

And remember that a child is like an unfinished painting. The day comes, often sadly, sometimes joyously, when we must hand the brush over and let him complete the masterpiece of a life lived.

Most teenagers, given guidance but allowed to look and learn about other faiths are grateful to those who permitted them the dignity of thinking for themselves.

WHAT ABOUT TEENS & THE INTERNET?

A fear of teen recruitment into religions via the Internet is generally unfounded. No studies or reliable reports show such occurring to any significant degree. Certainly the diversity of groups who have websites (from Druids to atheists) is enormous. But factually, probably no safer place exists to check out the beliefs or teachings of a group. The reader is secure in his own home, able to evaluate the information for himself against what he already knows and believes.

If you're concerned about what your child will see, get a block on their Internet access. Then sit down with them and search sites together via your log-on.

Banning a teen from checking out other beliefs or intriguing life questions will likely only make them more curious. A healthier approach might be to let them read the authorized websites of organizations and then discuss with them what was found and what questions they have.

examples #25-26

One woman's daughter found an occult group via the Internet. The girl began spending her nights with several other teens in blacked-out rooms, burning candles, while drinking tomato juice cocktails. Mom was concerned. But lucky for her daughter, Mom didn't panic. Instead she decided to do something positive.

She convinced the parents of all the other teens involved to form a committee. Each parent took on one day of the week to make sure the teens were involved in constructive life activities.

The room was soon repainted and the candles forgotten.

Distraught Wisconsin parents of a runaway daughter thought she had joined an "underground cult" in New York City. Local resources were contacted and the girl was located and her true situation sorted out. She had fallen in with the wrong crowd, lost her religious grounding, done things she was horribly ashamed of and didn't know how to tell her parents.

Much to the girl's relief, the parents chose a path of forgiveness and understanding. They expressed how much future the daughter still had. They told her how much they cared for her.

The family are now reconciled and working together on a positive direction for the daughter's life.

GET TO THE UNDERLYING PROBLEM

Thousands of parents have called our hotline with a loud and clear message of concern about kids involved in "cult" activity. Whether it is just dressing in black and wearing a pentagram or something more worrisome, the parents don't know how to change the apparently non-productive direction of their child's life.

Why do teens become involved in "dead-end activities" like Gangs, White Power, the illegal, the negative. Some experts tell us the biggest cause is lack of self-esteem. The kids think poorly of themselves. They see little value in their own lives and even less in others'.

"Lack of self-esteem" is neat and tidy psychobabble that therapists have spouted for years now. As though we could spot it in our kids and then dump a load of head pats, apologies, and flattery on them to cure what ails them.

No, it isn't that easy. People, young and old alike, "esteem" themselves — that is, they value themselves — or not — for good reason. For accomplishment. Rising to meet standards. Meeting moral demands. Achieving goals and purposes. Answering challenges placed on one by life. Delivering valuable service to one's family, company, or fellow man. Teens are no different. They know if they are meeting the expectations they have of themselves.

And what is one of the biggest failures that weighs on their minds and lies secretly behind the innocent eyes of so many teenagers?

Illiteracy.

Not test tube ideas about something that has traumatized them since the age of four.

No, it's much simpler.

They can't read.

They can't read and they hide it.

They hide it so they get no help.

They go on in school with their friends, but see their lives going nowhere.

What job offers?
What future?
What success?
For someone who can't read?

In a technological, computer-oriented society, young people realize quite early that unless they are literate they can't expect much of a future. Yet the problem of literacy is rarely addressed. The effects of illiteracy are far-reaching. It diminishes every decent prospect of the young person's life.

He may feel embarrassed, stupid, left out. Often he gets into some no-future activity — like "gothic."

Go to a Goth bar and ask how many people in the room have read a book in the last year. Don't be surprised if no tattooed arms shoot into the air.

Recognize and attack the right problem.

Find a remedial study program that goes back to basics. You want something that teaches phonics, that is, the sounds letters represent and how those sounds are put together to make words.

You want a book or study plan that helps them understand how such words are put together to make sentences and paragraphs. In short, find a program that really helps.

If no such programs are available locally, have your child read aloud to you. Sort out each word they have trouble with. Tell them how to pronounce it if need be. Explain the meaning of the word to them in simple terms until they graduate to using an easy dictionary. Keep this up and you will eventually have a child who can read comfortably. And with their increased literacy you will no doubt find self respect and, yes, self-esteem rising as well. Don't overlook illiteracy as a potential route to a destructive life path.

Give the gift of literacy to the young person who is involved in something absolutely valueless in the real world.

It is the road to a future of infinite possibilities. Of course, once you handle their literacy they may still be into the occult or something unusual. There are people who have earned their doctorate degrees who are experts in such. But they teach it at a university — they don't practice it at midnight in a blacked out bedroom while drinking tomato juice.

example #27

John was a teenager doing poorly in life and relationships. He was interviewed in depth about what was happening. He had become convinced that he was stupid and couldn't grasp what other young people were learning easily.

It turned out that while John understood the words which were being said around him, he was inundated with abbreviations that made no sense to him which others assumed he knew. This included many having to do with what he was studying.

He was amazed at how easy it was to clear up the things he didn't understand. And once this was done, it made a dramatic difference in his life and in his ability to interact with his friends.

Call our hotline (1-800-556-3055)

RELIGIOUS CONVERSION IS NOT BRAINWASHING.

Convincing someone to change their beliefs is not mind control. If it were, every religion in the world would be guilty of such.

In all the history of the United States, only one indictment was ever brought by federal prosecutors on the charge of brainwashing — a group of psychiatrists in Texas who used drugs, sleep deprivation and other horrors to make their victims think they had been "satanically abused" when no such thing had ever happened. The psychiatrists were fined millions and their clinic put out of business.

The term "brainwashing" stems from the Korean War era and also from the torture of political prisoners in the former Soviet Union. Men were brutalized, starved, drugged — any assault to weaken their resolve and change their loyalties. But it was discovered that once they escaped their oppressors, victims normally reverted to their former allegiances.

Mind control was similar. This was a concept investigated by the CIA and other intelligence agencies in the 1950s. LSD, combination pain-drug-hypnosis — all manner of things were tried. The CIA failed. Their dream of an army of programmed assassins died too. They eventually discovered that human minds don't control that easily, even after severe duress.

The terms "brainwashing" and "mind control" have, unfortunately, become misunderstood in the common man's eyes. **Hollywood and talk-show psychologists have given the impression that anyone's mind can be controlled almost hypnotically with very little effort.**

THE HOAX

BRAINWASHING & MIND CONTROL

We have been led to believe that any forceful or charismatic leader can mold us at will against our wishes and common sense. Thus "brainwashing" and "mind control" — once truly vicious and devastating methods — are now buzz phrases meaning any change of mind prompted by someone stronger or more clever. *This is a hoax.*

Do charismatic leaders exist? Absolutely. Can they be convincing to some people even when their ideas are illogical or strange? Certainly. Can they be strong-willed and clever? Yes. And some of their listeners can be foolish, weak-minded, easily deceived or lacking street smarts. But this is far from brainwashing or mind control. It is the selling of ideas through freedom of expression. This has been true throughout history. And it doesn't just happen in religion. Look at politics, advertising, business, and even personal relationships. **People pitch their ideas and sway minds in all walks of life.**

Brainwashing and mind control have been used as a simplistic explanation by some to explain why others would voluntarily take up certain beliefs. *Maybe it's simple, but it's wrong.*

The whole subject of brainwashing as it applies to religious groups has been debunked by competent scholars and repeated studies. Religious people do think for themselves. People who live in communes, people who become missionaries, or people who go to work for the Peace Corps. They are mostly idealistic souls who want to change the world for the better. Had our ancestors not thought similarly, we'd still be living in barbarism.

DIFFERENT AND DANGEROUS ARE NOT THE SAME THING.

All of today's main religions were radically different ideas when they came onto the world stage. And many viewed them as dangerous. **People often fear change.** We like the security of what we believe. Most of us feel that what we believe is "the way," as the Chinese call it — the right spiritual or philosophical path that leads to a happy life or salvation in the hereafter.

We want the same for our loved ones. We don't want to see them fall into a pit of false beliefs that will give them despair or doom their souls. These are honest desires. They are among our most decent impulses. To protect those dear to us. Indeed, to change the world by showing it "the way."

What irony that our most decent impulses can lead to our worst acts.

First we burn books, then heretics, then villages. Karl Marx, the father of communism, sarcastically pointed out this human weakness when he observed:

"The road to hell is paved with good intentions."

DIFFERENT

IS NOT DANGEROUS

We can fear that which is different and that which we don't understand. When we do, it becomes easier to accept false ideas about all kinds of new groups, about "brainwashing," or "mind control."

The message of intolerance, of the evil of anything different, may protect the status quo for the moment, but in the long run it may be the most dangerous message of all.

New ideas are regularly attacked. The story of Galileo — threatened by the Church for claiming the sun was the center of our solar system — is far from unique.

Religious scholars continually note that most religions begin as offshoots of older traditions, that followers of mainstream religions would do well to consider where they might be today if not for the independence of their own group's founders.

WHO WINS

WHEN RELIGION LOSES

The simple answer? No one.

Religion has had its shortcomings, to be sure. History has seen enough harm in the name of God and salvation.

But in the balance, religion prevails as a good and decent force for humanity. It addresses right and wrong conduct. It lifts man from the lion pit of day-to-day survival into realms of beauty and spirituality. It asks us to look at our responsibilities to our fellows.

These are not small things. In fact, we would have no civilization without them.

Most people recognize this. They feel there is something spiritual in man's relationship with the universe, its Creator or his fellow man. And most people want to know more about that spiritual connection.

There are canyon-deep questions — about the nature of man's soul, his true beginnings, his relationship to the wide universe and the Creator. They have been pondered through the ages by men of great learning and wisdom. Such will probably debate the answers for eons to come. But the majority of mankind seems to believe there is something more to man than his existence as a 98.6 F oxygen-burning machine. (Evidenced by the billions of Buddhists, Hindus, Muslims and Christians and countless others in the thousands of spiritual traditions of the earth.)

Whether that "something more" is labeled soul, spiritual being, elan vital, or the light within us all, this part of man needs to be addressed.

The world's religions have traditionally been the field which does so.

This serves all of us. Even non-believers benefit from the kindness and morality of the religious man.

The positive results are extensive. As one small example, expert studies have found that people with some religious grounding recover better from trauma and physical harm than those with none.

Unfortunately, there are certain schools of thought and therapy, even some which have gained prominance in some circles, whose basic tenets either ignore or denigrate religion.

For instance, Sigmund Freud is quoted as calling religion, "the universal neurosis of humanity."

One almost gets the impression from such people that religion has been proven to be a universal falsehood. These individuals sell personal anti-religious views under the cloak of science. Frankly, it is a shameful practice.

Anti-religious people often have little grasp of the uplift that moral and spiritual betterment gives an individual. They sometimes rail against religious practices they really don't understand.

This serves no one.

There is no evidence that no religion is good for one. There is plenty of evidence that some religion is.

It is important to be wary of religion haters when seeking advice.

How can you decide whether a counselor or advisor is qualified to help you in religious/spiritual matters? Choose someone who has an understanding of religions and who can tolerate religious diversity. He doesn't have to agree with you or even be a member of your faith. But take the time to ask about his or her background, views, leanings.

When searching for counseling on spiritual matters, it is essential to deal with a person who has spiritual grounding. You wouldn't ask a vegetarian to be the head chef at the annual banquet of the Cattleman's Association.

example #28

Below are excerpts from an infamous list of *"Conditions of Thought Reform"* which have been used to label religious groups as dangerous by psychiatrists and psychologists. Alongside are examples of positive groups we think fall quite clearly within these conditions.

"Typical Thought Reform Conditions"

Sample Groups
which exemplify such activity:

1. Keep the person unaware of what is going on and how she or he is being changed a step at a time...

> Kids who watch "Sesame Street"
> Foreign Exchange students
> Women who take classes to
>   learn about football
> Brownies/Cub Scouts
> Catholic catechism class attendees

2. Control the person's social and /or physical environment; especially control the person's time.

> Kindergarten
> Marine boot camp
> Weekend Christian retreat
> Weight loss health spa
> Boy Scout Jamboree

3. ...speak an in-group language...

> Doctors and nurses
> Computer whiz-kids
> Airline pilots
> Lawyers
> Sports fans

4. ...Manipulation of experiences can be accomplished through... long prayer sessions and lectures.

> Sunday morning Protestant
>   church services
> Catholic services in Latin
> College sociology lectures
> "60 Minutes" television show

"Typical Thought Reform Conditions"

Sample Groups
which exemplify such activity:

5. Manipulate a system of rewards, punishments...in order to promote...group-approved behavior

Parents of children anywhere on earth Nursery school teachers Sales team leaders

6. Put forth a closed system of logic and an authoritarian structure that permits no feedback and refuses to be modified by leadership approval or executive order. The group has a top-down, pyramid structure. The leaders must have verbal ways of never losing.

Office of the President of the United States British Royal Family Teamsters Union Any Political Party's National Committee Professional Football Team Owners

TOLERANCE. RELIGIOUS FREEDOM.

America's forefathers fought and died to make a country where those concepts could become reality.

We are infinitely better for it. But still we squabble like children. We need to learn to get along with each other. Judgment needs to be applied. Religious freedom cannot equate to lack of responsibility.

Because your beliefs are tolerated does not give one a license for injustice, hate speech or bigotry. It's funny that our religious zeal often prompts our worst hypocrisy. While most religious training promotes the kind treatment of others, we often interpret that to mean others of our own kind. Somehow, we don't see the Sermon on the Mount as applying to Chinese or Moslems. So we love our fellow Pentecostal but curse the Catholics at the dinner table.

Yet the great wisdom in our great religions almost universally tries to teach tolerance.

Maybe you do think all the Hindus and Buddhists are going to Hell.

Perhaps you see Oriental philosophies as just plain heathenism. Fine. You don't have to agree with these people. You can tell them so.

But neither does it serve to wholly condemn these strangers. To do so makes them "other" than you. It makes them seem less human. It becomes OK to lie about them, harm them, or even kill them because they are not like you.

Yet if you lived in their homes or spoke their language, you would see they laugh and cry like you. They love children. They tell jokes. They feel sorry for the unfortunate. They are, in fact, quite human and generally quite decent at heart.

IT'S O.K.

TO JUDGE — USE THE RIGHT CRITERIA

Tolerance cannot happen in an atmosphere of:

1. *Refusing to have any part of a group or organization because of differences in belief — despite evidence the organization is making a positive contribution to society.*

2. *Judging other people by how they think and what they believe — rather than on their actions and results.*

3. *Trying to convince people that others are bad through innuendo, half truths and even outright lies. Sometimes, sadly, the true motives in attempting to destroy one group is another group's effort to stop the first from threatening their own monopoly or funding.*

4. *Spreading fear-inciting propaganda about "brainwashing" and "mind control" which is not only disproven scientifically, but is reminiscent of the Salem witch hunts.*

It is OK to judge people and groups. Judge them by the results they produce. Do they promote peace and goodwill? Or are they labeling and marginalizing people? Are they exclusionary rather then inclusionary? If they were running the world, would you feel safe?

DON'T JUST FROWN ON RELIGIOUS INTOLERANCE.

Work to change it for the better. Help make that type of thinking and activity unpopular.

Join a religious tolerance organization.

Get involved in chat groups on the Internet.

Write editorials.

Start a Sunday morning radio talk show with a Muslim friend about common moral values.

Put up an Internet site — "Common Moral Values of Religions Around the World".

Work with any kind of betterment organization — religious, human rights, educational. Thousands of organizations are trying to improve things.

DO SOMETHING ABOUT IT —
EXPAND
YOUR HORIZONS

Support diversity education.

Many Sunday School classes run a program to visit other churches and enable their young people to learn about other faiths.

Work in the political arena, on legislative issues that deal with tolerance.

THE POSSIBILITIES ARE INFINITE.

IN CLOSING

This handbook may have given you different ideas than you expected.

We hope you will heed our advice to respect the beliefs of others and work out differences amicably.

As we said earlier —

THE RICHNESS OF DIVERSITY IS A WEALTH WE ALL SHARE.

Revel in it.

NOTES:

APPENDICES FOR REFERENCE

A) The first amendment to the Constitution of the United States of America

The first ten amendments are known as the Bill of Rights.

Amendment 1
FREEDOM OF RELIGION, SPEECH, PRESS, ASSEMBLY, AND PETITION (1791)

Congress shall make no law respecting an establishment of religion, or prohibiting the free exercise thereof; or abridging the freedom of speech, or of the press; or the right of the people peaceably to assemble, and to petition the Government for a redress of grievances.

B) Article 18 of the Universal Declaration of Human Rights

UNIVERSAL DECLARATION OF HUMAN RIGHTS
PREAMBLE

Whereas recognition of the inherent dignity and of the equal and inalienable rights of all members of the human family is the foundation of freedom, justice and peace in the world,

Whereas disregard and contempt for human rights have resulted in barbarous acts which have outraged the conscience of mankind, and the advent of a world in which human beings shall enjoy freedom of speech and belief and freedom from fear and want has been proclaimed as the highest aspiration of the common people,

Whereas it is essential, if man is not to be compelled to have recourse, as a last resort, to rebellion against tyranny and oppression, that human rights should be protected by the rule of law,

Whereas it is essential to promote the development of friendly relations between nations,

Whereas the peoples of the United Nations have in the Charter reaffirmed their faith in fundamental human rights, in the dignity and worth of the human person and in the equal rights of men and women and have determined to promote social progress and better standards of life in larger freedom,

Whereas Member States have pledged themselves to achieve, in cooperation with the United Nations, the promotion of universal respect for and observance of human rights and fundamental freedoms,

Whereas a common understanding of these rights and freedoms is of the greatest importance for the full realization of this pledge,

Now, therefore,
The General Assembly
proclaims
This Universal Declaration of Human Rights

as a common standard of achievement for all peoples and all nations, to the end that every individual and every organ of society, keeping this Declaration constantly in mind, shall strive by teaching and education to promote respect for these rights and freedoms and by progressive measures, national and international, to secure their universal and effective recognition and observance, both among the peoples of Member States themselves and among the peoples of territories under their jurisdiction...

Article 18 (of 30 articles)

Everyone has the right to freedom of thought, conscience and religion; this right includes freedom to change his religion or belief, and freedom, either alone or in community with others and in public or private, to manifest his religion or belief in teaching, practice, worship and observance.

G.A. res. 217A (III), U.N. Doc A/810 at 71 (1948)

Adopted on December 10, 1948
by the General Assembly of the United Nations
(without dissent)

C) UNITED STATES CODE - Title 18 Crimes and Criminal Procedure

Part I - Crimes
Chapter 13 - Civil Rights
Section 245 - Federally Protected Activities

(b) Whoever, whether or not acting under color of law, by force or threat of force willfully injures, intimidates or interferes with, or attempts to injure, intimidate or interfere with - ...

    (2) any person because of his race, color, religion or national origin ...

    (4) any person because he is or has been, or in order to intimidate such person or any other person or any class of persons from -

        (A) participating, without discrimination on account of race, color, religion or national origin, in any of the benefits or activities described in sub paragraphs (1)(A) through (1)(E) or subparagraphs (2)(A) through (2)(F); or (B) affording another person or class of persons opportunity or protection to so participate; or

(5) any citizen because he is or has been, or in order to intimidate such citizen or any other citizen from lawfully aiding or encouraging other persons to participate, with out discrimination on account of race, color, religion or national origin, in any of the benefits or activities described in subparagraphs (1)(A) through (1)(E) or sub paragraphs (2)(A) through (2)(F), or participating lawfully in speech or peaceful assembly opposing any denial of the opportunity to so participate

- shall be fined under this title, or imprisoned not more than one year, or both; and if bodily injury results from the acts committed in violation of this section or if such acts include the use, attempted use, or threatened use of a dangerous weapon, explosives, or fire shall be fined under this title, or imprisoned not more than ten years, or both; and if death results from the acts committed in violation of this section or if such acts include kidnapping or an attempt to kidnap, aggravated sexual abuse or an attempt to commit aggravated sexual abuse, or an attempt to kill, shall be fined under this title or impris- oned for any term of years or for life, or both, or may be sentenced to death. As used in this section, the term "participating lawfully in speech or peaceful assembly" shall not mean the aiding, abetting, or inciting of other persons to riot or to commit any act of physical violence upon any individual or against any real or personal property ...

ABOUT THE FOUNDATION

The Foundation for Religious Freedom is a tax-exempt non-profit religious tolerance organization run by a multi-faith Board of Directors.

We specialize in reconciling families and salvaging relationships. The more than 10,000 calls to our hotline in less than three years and the many hundreds of families we have helped work out their problems despite deep belief differences are ample evidence of this.

Our network of more than 200 experts includes pastors, college professors and deans (who have thousands of hours of study of the world's religions between them), attorneys of many faiths (who have defended the rights of a wide variety of religions to practice their beliefs freely), and religious liberty advocates from around the world who daily answer media inquiries and help families.

Beyond the daily work of saving families, the Foundation interfaces with dozens of other hotlines also intent on helping. It also coordinates with law enforcement bodies from the Los Angeles anti-terrorist unit to the FBI. It uses its network of experts to provide correct information and prevent tragedy caused by hate-speech or falsehoods.

The Foundation is also involved with local, national and international interfaith/world peace organizations from the United Religions Initiative, to the North American Interfaith Network to the Council for a Parliament for the World's Religions.

The Foundation believes the future belongs to people of compassion who embrace freedom of conscience, celebrate religious diversity and understand that the many faith traditions of the world enrich us all.

Board of Directors
Foundation for Religious Freedom

Book Design: Pamela Fraser/Blacktop Films
Email: ariel@primenet.com

RECOMMENDED ADDITIONAL READING AND VIEWING

Video:

Filmmaker Julia Pimsleur tells her family's story in
"Brother Born Again"

An uplifiting film for anyone who loves someone who has chosen another way of life, who has suspected a religion is a cult, or who thinks family ties should overcome differences.

Brother Born Again is an intimate documentary about Julia Pimsleur's attempt to reconnect with her only brother, Marc, a born-again Christian who lives with his spiritual family on a remote island in Alaska. The Pimsleur family feared Marc had joined a cult, and in the ten years since his conversion, a deep rift has formed between them. Family dynamics - as well as the definition of family itself - are explored as Julia, a Jewish woman living in New York, travels to Alaska to find out what made her sibling drop out of college and convert to a new faith and way of life.

Brother Born Again is the latest release from Big Mouth Productions (producers of "Nuyorican Dream" and "Innocent Until Proven Guilty," shown on Cinemax/Reel Life and HBO Signature).

Brother Born Again, a 76 min. documentary directed by Julia Pimsleur produced by Big Mouth Productions

__ $24.98 for individuals (including shipping)
__ $99.00 for institutions (including shipping)

please send a check and return mailing address to:
Big Mouth Productions
443 Broadway 5th floor
NY NY 10013
fax (212) 343-2609
or email us at
Big-Mouth-Prod@mindspring.com

(sorry, no credit cards)
we will send you a receipt by mail
please allow 2-3 weeks for delivery (rush requests are possible)

Book:

"New Religious Movements"
by George D. Chryssides
ISBN - 0304 336521

Objective and Informative

It would be easy for anyone embarking on a exploration
into new religious movements to be swayed by the sensa-
tionalist media reporting that many of these groups have
been subjected to. This book, however, deals with a host of
faiths and belief systems in a subjective and unbiased
way, however bizarre they appear to be. Even Jim Jones
gets a fair hearing!

A great source of information for anyone interested in
NRM's (New Religious Movements) which whets the
appetite for further study
Reviewer: S.A. Rivers, Port Soif, Vale, Guernsey United
Kingdom, 4 September 2000